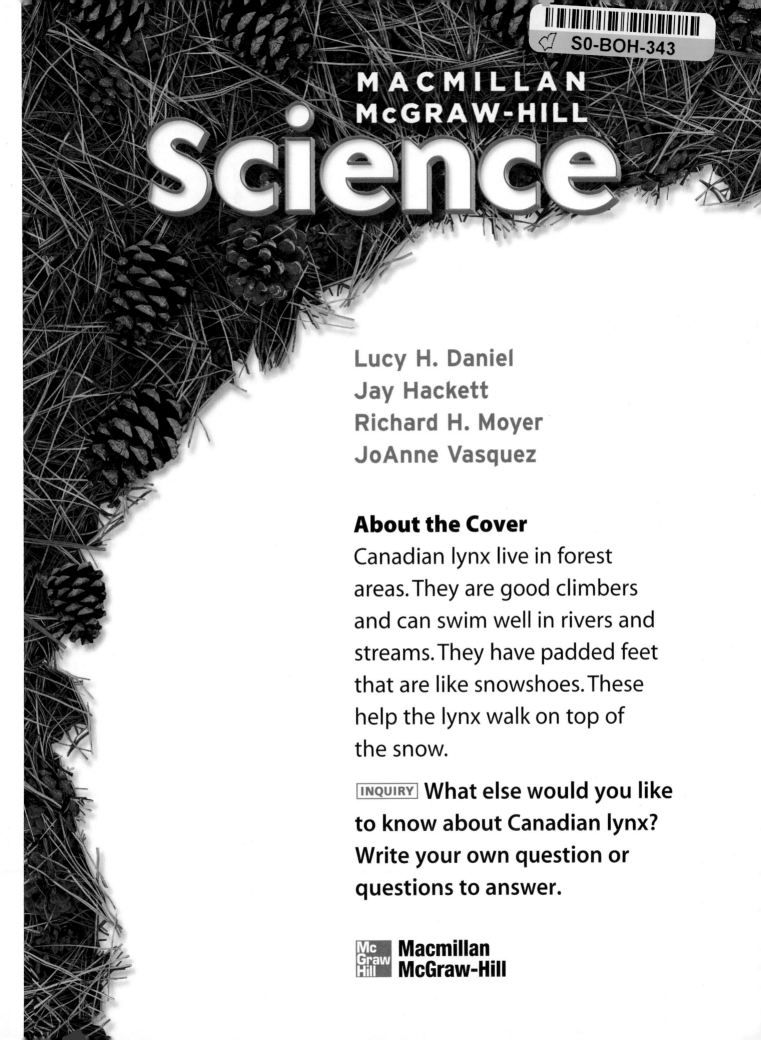

MACMILLAN McGRAW-HILL
Science

Lucy H. Daniel

Jay Hackett

Richard H. Moyer

JoAnne Vasquez

About the Cover

Canadian lynx live in forest areas. They are good climbers and can swim well in rivers and streams. They have padded feet that are like snowshoes. These help the lynx walk on top of the snow.

INQUIRY **What else would you like to know about Canadian lynx? Write your own question or questions to answer.**

Macmillan McGraw-Hill

Program Authors

Dr. Lucy H. Daniel
Teacher, Consultant
Rutherford County Schools, North Carolina

Dr. Jay Hackett
Professor Emeritus of Earth Sciences
University of Northern Colorado

Dr. Richard H. Moyer
Professor of Science Education
University of Michigan-Dearborn

Dr. JoAnne Vasquez
Elementary Science Education Consultant
Mesa Public Schools, Arizona
NSTA Past President

Contributing Authors

Lucille Villegas Barrera, M.Ed.
Elementary Science Supervisor
Houston Independent School District
Houston, Texas

Mulugheta Teferi, M.A.
St. Louis Public Schools
St. Louis, Missouri

Dinah Zike, M.Ed.
Dinah Might Adventures LP
San Antonio, Texas

The features in this textbook entitled "Amazing Stories," as well as the unit openers, were developed in collaboration with the National Geographic Society's School Publishing Division.

Copyright © 2002 National Geographic Society. All rights reserved.

learning through listening

Students with print disabilities may be eligible to obtain an accessible, audio version of the pupil edition of this textbook. Please call Recording for the Blind & Dyslexic at 1-800-221-4792 for complete information.

The McGraw·Hill Companies

Macmillan
McGraw-Hill

Published by Macmillan/McGraw-Hill, of McGraw-Hill Education, a division of The McGraw-Hill Companies, Inc., Two Penn Plaza, New York, New York 10121.

Printed in the United States of America
ISBN 0-02-282589-4/2

4 5 6 7 8 9 027/043 09 08 07 06

Teacher Reviewers

Michelle Dunning
Birmingham, Alabama

Donna Bullock
Chandler, Arizona

Debra Allen
Davie, Florida

Lora Meade
Plantation, Florida

Roxanne Laird
Miami, Florida

Karen Gaudy
Satellite Beach, Florida

Stephanie Sirianni
Margate, Florida

Heidi Stephens
South Daytona, Florida

Rosanne Phillips
Miami, Florida

Brenda Crow
Miami, Florida

Kari Pingel
Pella, Iowa

Christie Jones
Springfield, Illinois

Diane Songer
Wabash, Indiana

Lee Arwood
Wabash, Indiana

Margarite Hart
Indianapolis, Indiana

Charlotte Bennett
Newburgh, Indiana

Donna Halverson
Evansville, Indiana

Stephanie Tanke
Crown Point, Indiana

Mindey LeMoine
Marquette, Michigan

Billie Bell
Grand View, Missouri

Charlotte Sharp
Greenville, North Carolina

Pat Shane
Chapel Hill, North Carolina

Karen Daniel
Chapel Hill, North Carolina

Linda Dow
Concord, North Carolina

Consultants

Dr. Carol Baskin
University of Kentucky
Lexington, KY

Dr. Joe W. Crim
University of Georgia
Athens, GA

Dr. Marie DiBerardino
Allegheny University of
Health Sciences
Philadelphia, PA

Dr. R. E. Duhrkopf
Baylor University
Waco, TX

Dr. Dennis L. Nelson
Montana State University
Bozeman, MT

Dr. Fred Sack
Ohio State University
Columbus, OH

Dr. Martin VanDyke
Denver, CO

Dr. E. Peter Volpe
Mercer University
Macon, GA

Consultants

Dr. Clarke Alexander
Skidaway Institute of
Oceanography
Savannah, GA

Dr. Suellen Cabe
Pembroke State University
Pembroke, NC

Dr. Thomas A. Davies
Texas A & M University
College Station, TX

Dr. Ed Geary
Geological Society of America
Boulder, CO

Dr. David C. Kopaska-Merkel
Geological Survey of Alabama
Tuscaloosa, AL

Consultants

Dr. Bonnie Buratti
Jet Propulsion Lab
Pasadena, CA

Dr. Shawn Carlson
Society of Amateur Scientists
San Diego, CA

Dr. Karen Kwitter
Williams College
Williamstown, MA

Dr. Steven Souza
Williamstown, MA

Dr. Joseph P. Straley
University of Kentucky
Lexington, KY

Dr. Thomas Troland
University of Kentucky
Lexington, KY

Dr. Josephine Davis Wallace
University of North Carolina
Charlotte, NC

Consultant for Primary Grades

Donna Harrell Lubcker
East Texas Baptist University
Marshall, TX

Teacher Reviewers (continued)

Beth Lewis
Wilmington, North Carolina

Cindy Hatchell
Wilmington, North Carolina

Cindy Kahler
Carrboro, North Carolina

Diane Leusky
Chapel Hill, North Carolina

Heather Sutton
Wilmington, North Carolina

Crystal Stephens
Valdese, North Carolina

Meg Millard
Chapel Hill, North Carolina

Patricia Underwood
Randleman, North Carolina

E. Joy Mermin
Chapel Hill, North Carolina

Yolanda Evans
Wilmington, North Carolina

Tim Gilbride
Pennsauken, New Jersey

Helene Reifowitz
Nesconsit, New York

Tina Craig
Tulsa, Oklahoma

Deborah Harwell
Lawton, Oklahoma

Kathleen Conn
West Chester, Pennsylvania

Heath Renninger Zerbe
Tremont, Pennsylvania

Patricia Armillei
Holland, Pennsylvania

Sue Workman
Cedar City, Utah

Peg Jensen
Hartford, Wisconsin

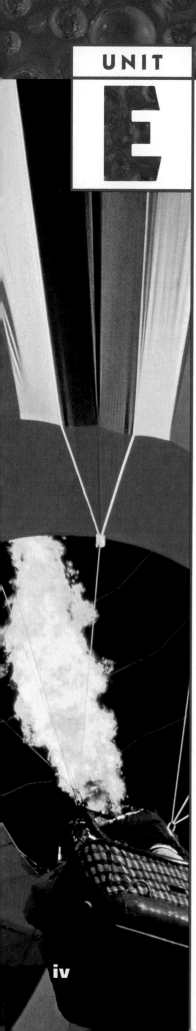

Matter and Energy PAGE E1

For Your Reference

Skills Handbook

Science Handbook

Health Handbook

Activities

Unit E

Explore Activities

Links

UNIT E

Matter and Energy

LOOK!

Have you ever seen this kind of balloon? Do you know what makes these balloons move through the air? Take a good look.

Matter and Energy

Matter

Vocabulary

matter, E6

mass, E7

property, E8

temperature, E9

solid, E12

liquid, E14

volume, E15

gas, E16

physical change, E20

chemical change, E22

Did You Ever Wonder?

How do these wind surfers use all three forms of matter? The surfboard is a solid. It floats on top of water, a liquid. Air is a gas that pushes the wind surfer forward.

INQUIRY SKILL **Communicate** how we use matter at school and home.

E 3

Matter All Around

Get Ready

Have you ever been to a party? Suppose you were at the party in this picture. What could you see, hear, smell, and touch?

Inquiry Skill

You **observe** when you use your senses to learn about something.

Explore Activity

How can you tell what is inside?

What to do

1 **Observe** each container without opening it.

2 Predict what is inside each one. Make a chart.

3 Open each container. Did you predict correctly?

4 FURTHER INQUIRY How did you **observe** what was inside?

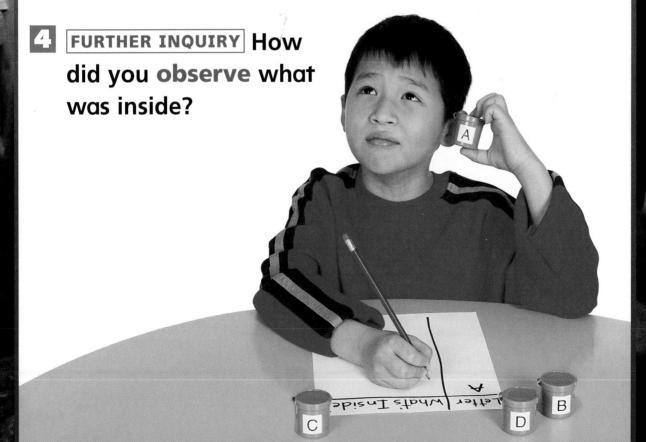

How are all things alike?

All things are made of **matter**. Matter is anything that takes up space. Observe the objects in this room. They are all made of matter. You are made of matter, too.

The air in these balloons is matter.

These stuffed animals are matter.

All matter also has **mass**. Mass is how much matter is in an object. A bed has a lot of mass. A goldfish has only a little mass.

▷ **How is everything in this room alike?**

This boy is matter.

This metal can is matter.

The water in this tank is matter.

How can you describe matter?

You use your senses to describe matter. You can describe matter by its properties. A **property** tells you something about an object. Some properties of matter are shape, size, color, and smell. Matter can sink or float. This is also a property.

big, soft

red, shiny

floats

sinks

Temperature measures how warm something is. Temperature is a property of matter.

Texture tells the way something feels. Texture is another property of matter.

hot

fuzzy   smooth

▶ **What are some other properties of this stuffed frog?**

Think and Write

1. What is matter?

2. Name something that has a lot of mass. Name something that has a little mass.

3. Name three properties of matter.

LOG ON Visit www.science.mmhschool.com to learn more about matter.

Three States of Matter

Get Ready

Matter is everywhere! What kinds of matter do you see in this picture? Which things have the most mass? Which things have the least mass?

Inquiry Skill

You put things **in order** when you tell what is first, next, and last.

Explore Activity

How can you put matter in order?

What to do

1 Which object has the most mass? The least? Predict.

2 Compare two objects on the balance. The one that makes the pan go lower has more mass.

3 Put the objects **in order** from least mass to most mass.

4 FURTHER INQUIRY Use a ruler to measure each object. How else can you put the objects **in order**?

What is a solid?

There are three different states of matter. **Solid** is one state of matter. Like all matter, a solid takes up space and has mass. But only a solid has a shape of its own. Things made out of metal, plastic, and wood are solids.

yo-yo

in-line skate

Crayon

pocket game

feather

E 12

You can measure the shape of a solid. A ruler is a tool that measures how long, wide, or high things are. This ruler measures centimeters. Some rulers measure inches.

ruler

You can measure the mass of a solid. A balance is a tool that measures mass. The side of the balance that is lower holds the thing that has more mass.

balance

How are all of these objects alike?

What is a liquid?

Liquid is another state of matter. A liquid takes up space and has mass. A liquid does not have a shape of its own. It takes the shape of its container. Milk, juice, and water are all liquids.

oil

liquid soap

milk

juice

Volume is the amount of space that something takes up. You can measure the volume of a liquid. A measuring cup is one way to measure volume. A measuring cup can hold the same amount of liquid every time.

▶ **How can you measure the volume of this punch?**

Cranberry Juice

E 15

What is a gas?

The third state of matter is **gas**. It takes up space and has mass. Gas spreads out to fill its container. It does not have a shape of its own.

Air is made up of gases. You can not see it, but air is everywhere. It can fill up a tire or a ball.

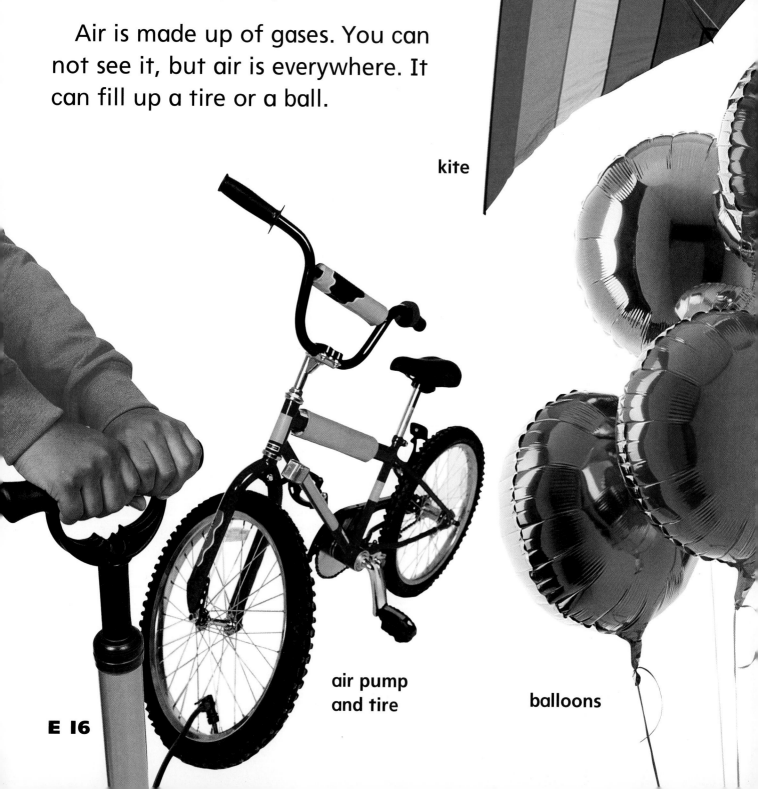

kite

air pump and tire

balloons

When you blow up a ball, gas fills the inside. Gas pushes out the sides and makes the ball bigger.

When a gas is heated, it spreads out. It fills more of its container. When a gas is cooled, it spreads out less. It fills less of its container.

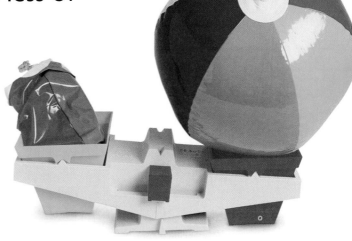

▶ **Where is gas in each of these pictures?**

Think and Write

1. What are three states of matter?

2. What kind of matter is an ice cube?

3. What kind of matter is air?

MORE TO READ

Read **Solids, Liquids, and Gases** by Louise Osborne, Deborah Hodge, and Ray Boudreau.

Changing Matter

Have you ever put two or more things together to make something new? Look at this work of art. How would you make something like this?

Inquiry Skill

You **investigate** when you make a plan and try it out.

Explore Activity

How can you change matter?

What you need

glue

paper

scissors

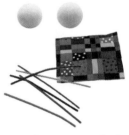

craft materials

What to do

1 Observe your objects.

2 **Investigate** how to change and put together the objects. Make a plan and try it out.

BE CAREFUL! Scissors are sharp.

3 What did you make? What did you do to make it? Tell how you changed matter.

4 **FURTHER INQUIRY** **Investigate** how water can change matter. What happens when you wet your object?

What is physical change?

Matter may change in different ways. You can change the size or shape of matter. This is called a **physical change**.

In a physical change, you can cut, fold, bend, or tear matter. When you only change the shape of matter, its mass stays the same.

You can also change matter by mixing it. A mixture is made of two or more different things. You can mix solids, liquids, and gases. You can separate them from a mixture too.

Mixing is a physical change. When pieces of matter are mixed together, each piece is the same as it was before it was mixed.

The salad and salad dressing are both mixtures.

▷ **Which has more mass, a head of lettuce, or a head of lettuce torn into pieces?**

What is chemical change?

Sometimes matter can change into different matter. This is called a **chemical change**. When matter goes through a chemical change, its properties change.

Burning is a chemical change. It changes wood to ashes.

Rusting is a chemical change. Some metals can rust.

Baking is a chemical change. You can heat flour, milk, sugar, and eggs to make bread.

All matter does not change in the same way. The air can change the color of a fruit. An apple will turn brown. Water and air can cause iron to rust. They can not cause plastic to change.

Before	After

▷ **What happens when something goes through a chemical change?**

Think and Write

1. Name a physical change.

2. What is a mixture?

3. Name a chemical change.

LOG ON Visit www.science.mmhschool.com to learn more about how matter can change.

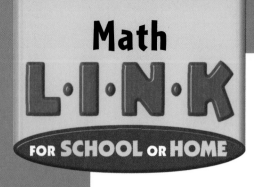
Take a Closer Look

Some objects are made of small parts. Scientists use microscopes and hand lenses to observe them. You can use two hand lenses to look at objects. Hold one hand lens above the other one and observe.

Try This!

Practice using hand lenses. Observe cloth, hair, or paper. Then use hand lenses to observe seeds inside fruits. How many seeds do you see? Record the numbers in a bar graph.

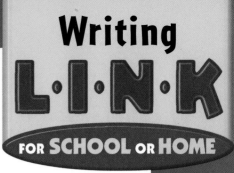
Write a Secret Note

Dip a cotton swab into a glass of milk or lemon juice. Write a message on white paper with the cotton swab. Let the note dry. Then hold the note up to a window on a sunny day. Watch to see what happens!

Try This!

Writing That Explains Write a letter to a friend. Explain how to write a secret note. Ask your friend to tell you what happens.

Chapter 9 Review

Vocabulary

chemical change, E22

gas, E16

liquid, E14

mass, E7

matter, E6

physical change, E20

property, E8

solid, E12

temperature, E9

volume, E15

Use each word once for items 1–9.

1 Anything that takes up space and has mass is _____ .

2 The amount of matter in an object is called its _____ .

3 The size, shape, or color of an object is a _____ of the object.

4 Matter that has a shape of its own is called a _____ .

5 Matter, such as juice, that has no shape of its own is called a _____ .

6 The amount of space something takes up is called its _____ .

7 Matter, such as air, that spreads out to fill its container is called a _____ .

8 The _____ is a measure of how hot something is.

9 Write which type of change each picture shows.

A

B

E 26

Science Ideas

Tell what kind of matter each picture shows.

10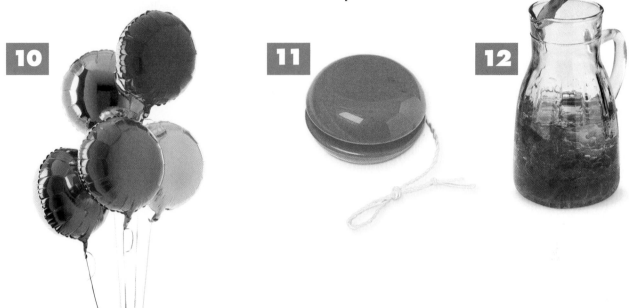

11

12

Inquiry Skill: Investigate

13 Write a plan for how you could change this clay by making only physical changes.

Did You Ever Wonder?

INQUIRY SKILL **Investigate** why chemical changes are important. What chemical changes happen when people cook?

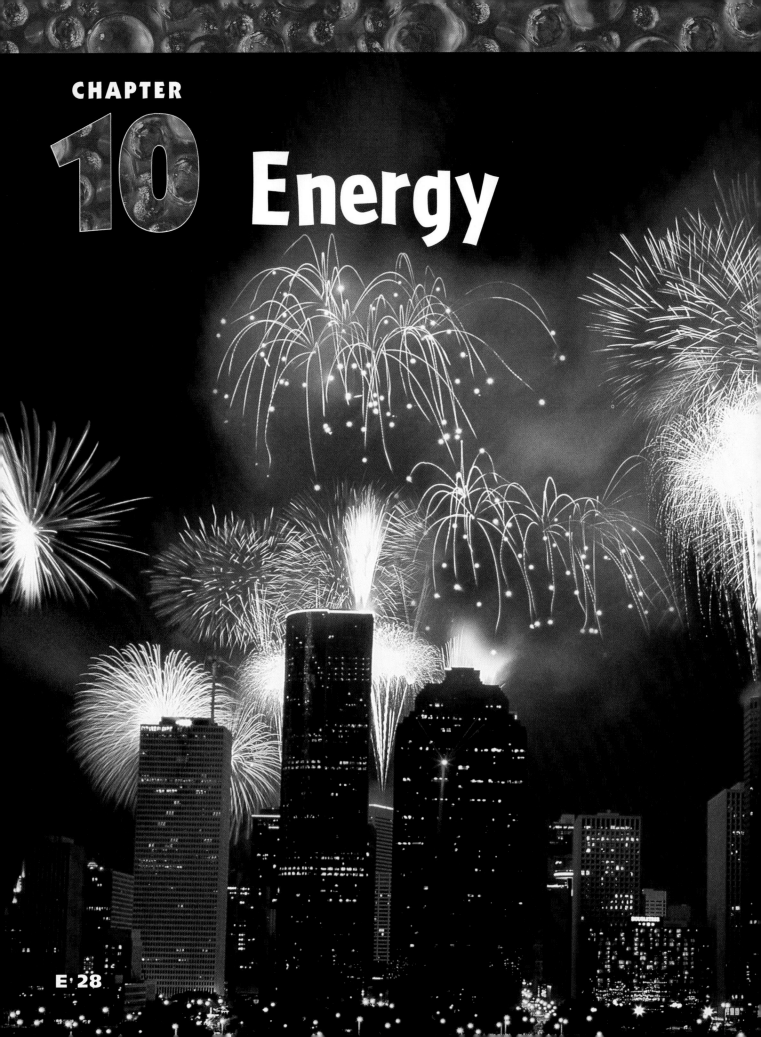

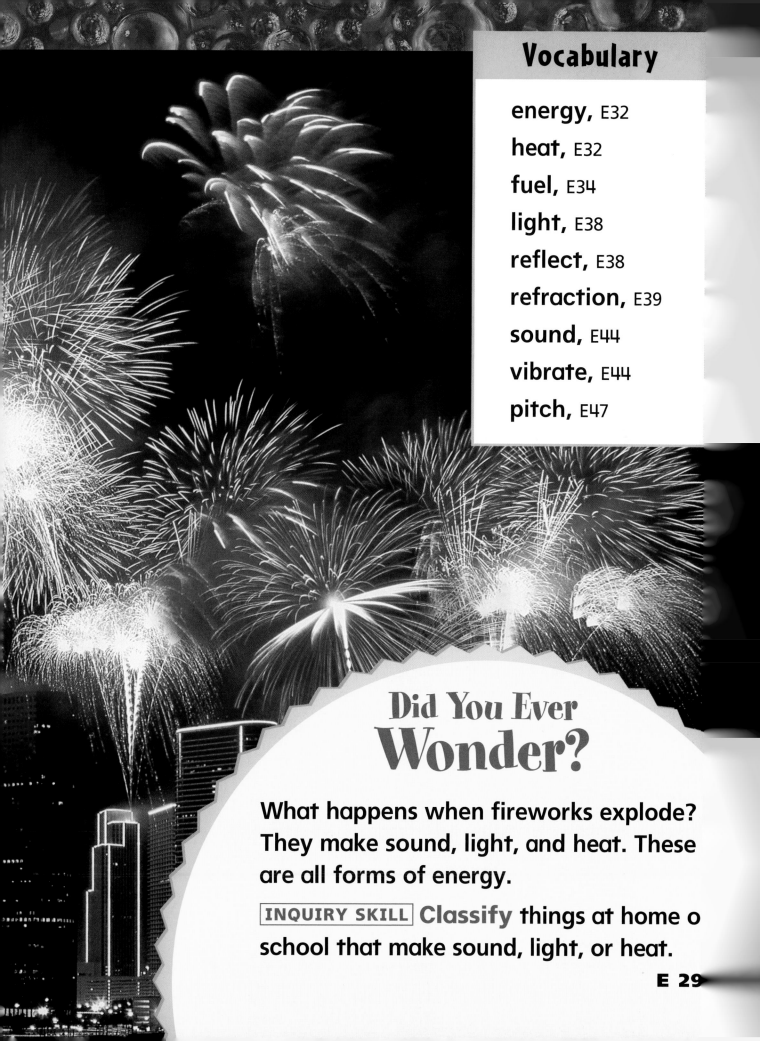

Did You Ever Wonder?

What happens when fireworks explode? They make sound, light, and heat. These are all forms of energy.

INQUIRY SKILL **Classify** things at home o school that make sound, light, or heat.

Heat

Get Ready

A cold treat is great on a hot day. But the treat won't last long. Look at the picture. What do you think makes this ice cream lose its shape? Tell your ideas to a partner.

Inquiry Skill

You **communicate** when you share your ideas with others.

Explore Activity

How can heat change matter?

What you need

paper plates

ice cube

butter

chocolate

What to do

1 Find a sunny spot. Place the ice cube, butter, and chocolate on the plates. Draw how they look.

2 How will the Sun change each item? Leave the paper plates in the Sun.

3 **Communicate** what happens to each item. Draw how they look. Compare your pictures.

4 FURTHER INQUIRY How did heat change matter? **Communicate** your ideas to a partner.

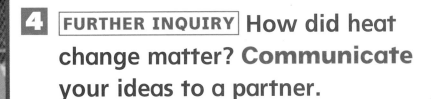

How can heat change matter?

Energy can make matter move or change. One kind of energy is heat. Heat can change matter from one state to another. Taking away heat can change a liquid to a solid. Adding heat can change a liquid to a gas. These changes are physical changes.

1

Water takes the shape of its container.

The tray is put in the freezer. The liquid will change to a solid state. The plastic tray will not change.

The solid ice cubes are placed in a pan and left at room temperature.

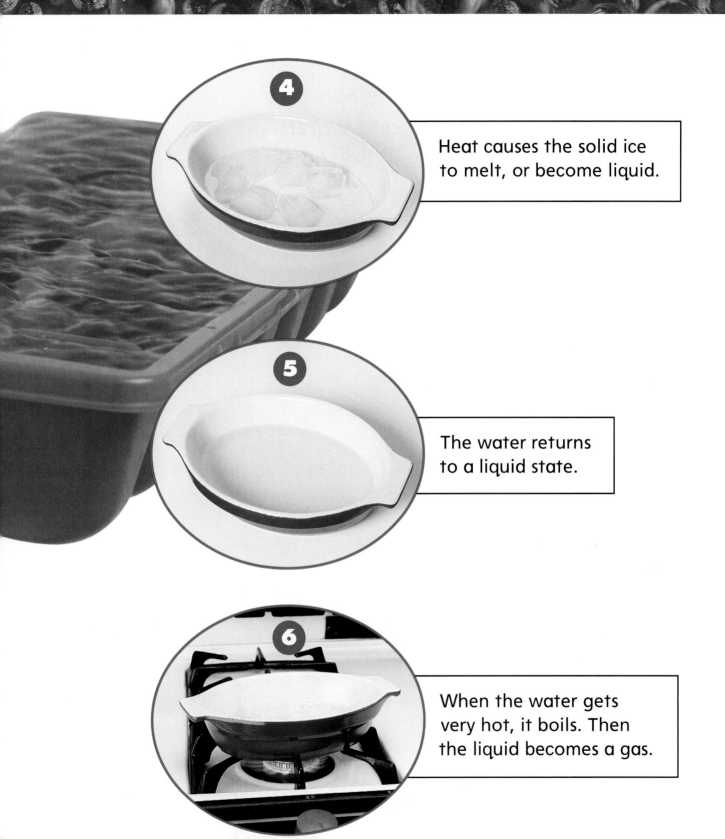

4 Heat causes the solid ice to melt, or become liquid.

5 The water returns to a liquid state.

6 When the water gets very hot, it boils. Then the liquid becomes a gas.

▶ **How can you change the state of water?**

How can we use heat?

Much of our heat is from the Sun. The Sun warms Earth's land, air, and water. Without the Sun, Earth would be too cold for things to live.

Fire gives off heat. To do this, it burns **fuel**. Wood, natural gas, and oil are fuels.

Heat can come from electricity, too. We can use dams on rivers to make electricity.

You can rub your hands to make heat. Then you can hold a pencil. The heat moves from your hand to the pencil. Heat can move from one object to another. Heat moves through metal quickly. That is why people use metal pans when they cook.

Heat can change things. When a potter puts clay in a special oven, it changes. It becomes very hard.

▶ **How is heat used in these pictures?**

Think and Write

1. Name two ways heat can change matter.

2. Where does much of our heat come from?

HOME ACTIVITY Put a tray of water and a wooden block in the freezer for two hours. What happens to each one?

Get Ready

Look at the buildings in this picture. What do you see? What direction is the light coming from?

Inquiry Skill

You **observe** when you use your senses to find out about something.

Explore Activity

How does light move?

flashlight

mirror

What to do

1 Stand near a wall with the flashlight. Have a partner hold the mirror.

2 Shine the flashlight at the mirror. Your partner will use the mirror to aim the light on the wall.

3 **Observe** what happens to the light. How does light move?

4 FURTHER INQUIRY Shine the flashlight on other objects. **Observe** how light moves.

What is light?

Light is a kind of energy that lets us see. Light travels in straight lines.

When light hits an object, some of it **reflects**, or bounces off, the object. When light reflects off smooth, flat objects like mirrors, it bounces in one direction.

This mirror is not flat. When light hits the surface, it bounces off in many directions. This makes your reflection look funny.

When an object blocks light, it makes a shadow. A shadow is a dark area that light does not reach. You can make a shadow on the wall by blocking light with your hand. Some objects do not block light. They do not make shadows.

Glass or water can bend light. This is called **refraction**. A hand lens bends light. Bending light can make something look bigger.

▷ **How does light travel?**

Light bends when it travels through this hand lens. Bent light makes the butterfly look bigger.

How do we use light?

Much of Earth's light is from the Sun. Living things need the energy from sunlight. Without the Sun, Earth would be in darkness. Nothing would be able to live or grow here.

People once used fire for light indoors and at night. Now we use electric lights to help us see.

▶ **How is light being used in these pictures?**

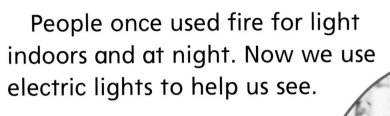

Think and Write

1. What is light?

2. How is a shadow made?

3. What gives us light energy after dark?

LOG ON Visit www.science.mmhschool.com to learn more about light.

Sound

Get Ready

Sounds are all around us.
Look closely at this picture.
How are these people
making sound? What do
you think it sounds like?

Inquiry Skill

You **observe** when you
use your senses to find
out about something.

Explore Activity

paper cup

string

goggles

paper clip

How is sound made?

What to do

1 Work with two partners. Make a tiny hole in the bottom of the cup. Tie the string to the paper clip. Pull the string through the hole.

2 Hold the cup and string with one partner. The other partner snaps the string. **BE CAREFUL!** Wear goggles.

3 **Observe** what happens. How did you make sound?

4 **FURTHER INQUIRY** Change the length of the string. **Observe** what happens. How does the sound change?

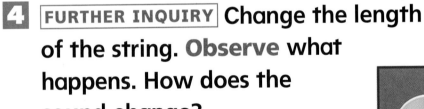

What is sound?

Sound is a kind of energy. Sound is made when something **vibrates**, or moves back and forth. When something vibrates it makes the air around it vibrate, too. Vibrating air moves to your ear. It makes part of your ear vibrate. That is how you hear.

When you speak, air from your lungs makes your vocal chords vibrate. Touch your throat as you speak. Feel the vibration.

Sound travels in waves. Sound waves move through the air like ripples in a pond.

▶ **What carries most of the sound you hear?**

What makes loud and soft sounds?

Not all sounds are the same. Some sounds are loud. Big vibrations make loud sounds. Some sounds are soft. Small vibrations make soft sounds. The farther away you are from a sound, the softer it sounds to you.

▷ **How would you compare the sound of a motorcycle to the sound of a bicycle?**

What is pitch?

Sounds can also be high, low, or somewhere in between. **Pitch** is how high or how low a sound is.

Musical instruments work by vibrating. Look at this instrument. When you hit a small bar, the vibrations are fast. The pitch is high. When you hit a big bar, the vibrations are slow. The pitch is low.

low pitch

> **How would you describe the pitch of each dog's bark?**

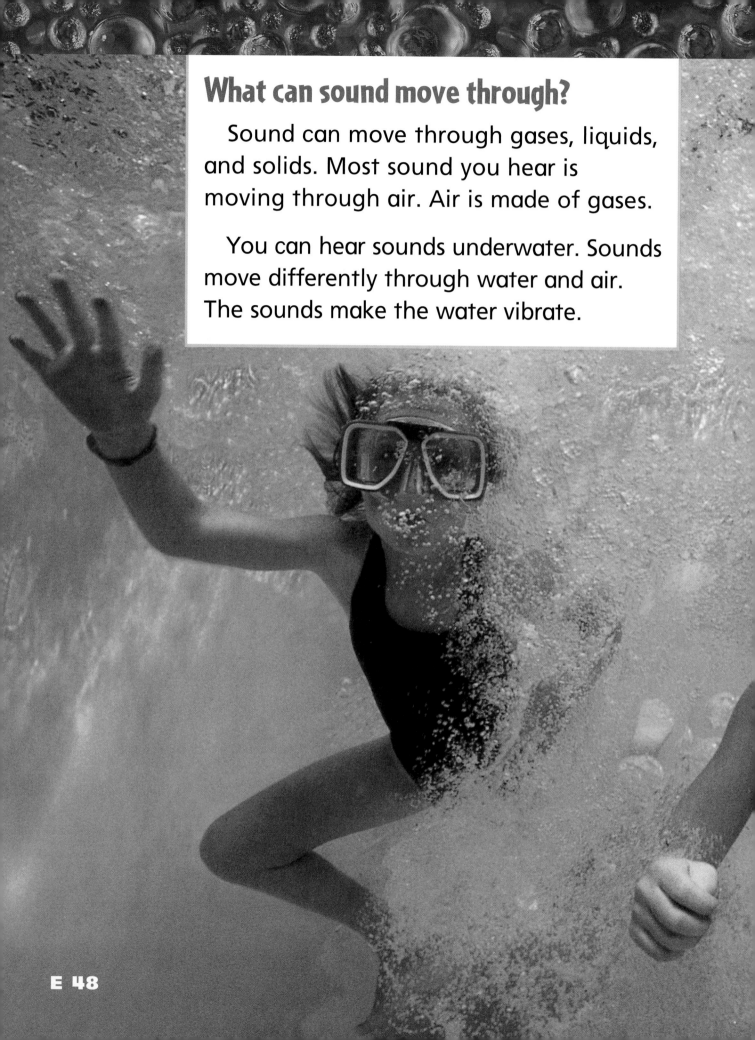

What can sound move through?

Sound can move through gases, liquids, and solids. Most sound you hear is moving through air. Air is made of gases.

You can hear sounds underwater. Sounds move differently through water and air. The sounds make the water vibrate.

Have you put your ear to a desk or a door and heard a sound from the other side? The sound makes the wood vibrate. The wood is a solid.

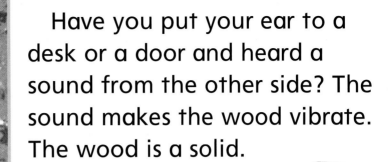

? What happens when sound travels through a solid?

Think and Write

1. How is sound made?

2. What is pitch?

3. Tell what sound can move through.

MORE TO READ Read **Energy** by Alvin Silverstein, Virginia Silverstein, and Laura Silverstein Nunn.

Thomas Alva Edison

by Tamera Bryant
illustrated by Laurie Jordan

McGraw Hill

Write About the Past

Think about what life was like before electric light bulbs. Read *Thomas Alva Edison* by Tamera Bryant. Think about all the things that Edison invented. How did they change people's lives?

Try This!

How would your life be different without Thomas Edison's inventions? Write a story about what your life might have been like.

Make Your Own Music

People have been making music for a very long time. The first instruments invented were probably hollow logs used as drums. You can invent your own instrument, too.

Try This!

Think of ways to make a musical instrument. Find things that can make sounds. Try to make sounds with high pitch and low pitch. Can you play a tune?

Science Newsroom CD-ROM Choose **Bouncing Sounds** to learn more about sound.

Chapter 10 Review

Vocabulary

energy, E32

fuel, E34

heat, E32

light, E38

pitch, E47

reflects, E38

refraction, E39

sound, E44

vibrates, E44

Use each word once for items 1–9.

1 When you make matter move or change you use ____ .

2 Energy that can change the state of matter is called ____ .

3 Something that gives off heat when it burns is ____ .

4 Energy that you hear is called ____ .

5 How high or low a sound is, is called its ____ .

6 When something moves back and forth quickly, it ____ .

7 Energy that allows you to see is called ____ .

8 When light bounces off a mirror, the mirror ____ the light.

9 When something bends light, it is called ____ .

Science Ideas

10 What can sound move through?

11 Which picture shows heat?

A

B

C

Inquiry Skill: Communicate

Tell what each of these pictures shows.

12

13

READ
Fossil Fuels Keep Us Warm by Shirley Granahan
Sending a Message with Dots...and Dashes... by Emily North

Did You Ever **Wonder?** | INQUIRY SKILL | **Investigate** loud and quiet sounds at school or home. How can loud sounds be helpful?

A GLOW-ING IDEA!

When Becky Schroeder was ten years old, she had a really bright idea. One afternoon, she was doing homework while in the car with her mom. Soon it got dark. Becky wanted to see what she was writing without turning on a light. So she invented a way to do it.

Becky Schroeder has dreamed up nine inventions.... This is one of them.

Becky Schroeder's Glo-sheet

Becky and her dad bought special paint that glowed after light hit it. Becky coated a clipboard with the paint and took the clipboard into a dark room. The board glowed . . . even through the piece of paper she had placed on top! Now she could write in the dark. Becky named her invention the Glo-sheet.

Young inventor Becky Schroeder

Write about something you would like to invent. Tell how it would be useful to people.

Matter, Matter Everywhere

Look at the object. What state of matter is the object? What are its properties? How can you make a physical change to it? How can you make a chemical change to it? Make a book to show your ideas.

Heat, Sound, and Light

Think of three objects that give off heat, sound, or light. Draw a picture of each. Then create an invention that uses heat, sound, or light. Write or tell what your invention does. How can it help people?

For Your Reference

Observe

You **observe** when you use your senses to learn about something. Your senses tell you how things look, sound, feel, smell, or taste.

pencil

crayons

paper

What to do

1 **Observe** something in the Science Center. How does it look? Feel? Smell? Sound?

2 Draw and write about it.

3 Tell a friend which of your senses helped you the most.

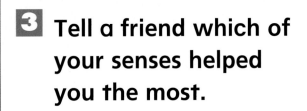

Inquiry Skill Builder 2

Measure

You can **measure** to find out how long, fast, or warm something is. You use numbers to record the answer.

warm and cold water

What to do

1 Fill one cup with warm water. Fill the other cup with cold water.

2 Place a thermometer in each cup. Wait 2 minutes. **Measure** the temperatures.

2 thermometers

3 Compare your temperatures with a partner's. Did you both get the same numbers? If not, measure again.

Compare

You **compare** things when you show how they are alike and different.

What you need

paper

pencil

What to do

1 **Compare** the people.

2 List three ways they are alike. List three ways they are different.

3 Choose an animal. How are the people different from the animal?

Inquiry Skill Builder 4

Classify

What you need

paper

pencil

You **classify** when you put things into groups to show how they are alike.

What to do

1 Look at the picture of the beans.

2 **Classify** the beans by size. How many are big? How many are small?

3 Find another way to classify the beans.

Make a Model

You **make a model** when you do something to show a place or thing. A model can help you learn how a place looks or how a thing works.

What to do

1 **Make a model** of a clock. Include numbers and hands.

BE CAREFUL! Scissors are sharp.

2 Tell what you can learn about a real clock from the model.

3 Tell how a real clock is different from the model.

What you need

paper

crayons

scissors

paper fastener

Inquiry Skill Builder 6

Communicate

You **communicate** when you talk, write, or draw to share your ideas.

What you need

paper

pencil

What to do

1 Think about your favorite food.

2 Write about it and draw a picture.

3 **Communicate** to a friend about your favorite food. Ask your friend to name the food you described.

Infer

To **infer**, you use what you know to figure something out.

What you need

paper

pencil

What to do

1 Look at the pictures. Record what you observe about each picture.

2 Use what you know to **infer** which place is warmer.

3 Write a short story to tell what people do to have fun in each place.

Put Things in Order

To put things **in order**, you tell what happens first, next, and last.

What to do

1 Think about all the things that you did this morning.

2 List the things on your paper. Write them **in order**.

3 Draw a picture of you doing one of those things.

What you need

pencil

crayons

paper

Predict

You **predict** when you use what you know to tell what you think will happen.

crayons

"I'm hungry," said Laura.

"Me, too," replied Jack.

"I wish I had a snack," Laura said.

"All I have are these grapes," said Jack.

paper

What to do

1 Read the story above.

2 **Predict** what will happen next.

3 Draw a picture to show it.

Investigate

When you **investigate**, you make a plan and try it out.

What to do

1 Use clay and pencils to make a shape.

2 How many blocks can your shape hold? **Investigate** to find out. Make a plan and try it.

3 Have a partner try your plan. How many blocks did your partner use? Did you use the same number?

What you need

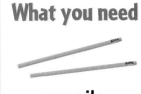
pencils

clay

blocks

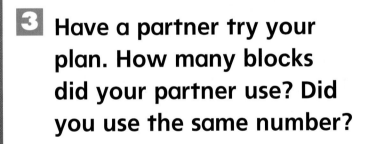

Draw a Conclusion

To **draw a conclusion**, you use what you observe to explain what happens.

What to do

1 Look at the picture. Where do you think the girl went? What do you think she did?

2 **Draw a conclusion.** Show it in a picture.

3 Explain your conclusion to a friend. Does your friend agree with you? Why or why not?

What you need

crayons

paper

Save and Recycle

We should not waste things.

Use no more
than you need.

Don't leave
the water on.

Recycle as much
as you can.

Use things more
than once.

Care of Animals

Here are ways to care for animals.

- Give pets food and water. Give them a safe place to live, too.

- Be kind to pets. Handle them with care.

- Don't touch wild animals. They may bite, sting, or scratch you.

- Do not touch things in places where wild animals live.

Care of Plants

Here are ways to care for plants.

- Give plants water and sunlight.

- Ask the teacher before you touch or eat a plant. Some plants can make you very sick!

- Do not dig up plants or pick flowers. Let plants grow where they are.

Clean Up

We need to keep work places clean.

Let an adult clean
up broken glass.

Pour water into a sink,
not into a trash can.

Put food in plastic bags.
This keeps bugs away.

Don't get paint
or food on you.

How to Measure

You can use objects to measure. Line up the objects and count them. Use objects that are alike. They must be the same size.

This string is about 8 paper clips long.

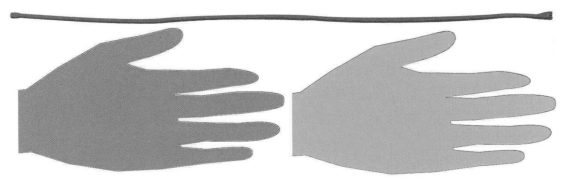

This string is about 2 hands long.

Try This!

- Measure some string. Tell how you did it.

- Can you measure string with these paper clips? Why or why not?

R 17

Measure in Centimeters

You can use a ruler to measure. You can use centimeters (cm). This is called a unit of measurement. You can measure this insect. Line up the end of the insect with the 0 on the ruler.

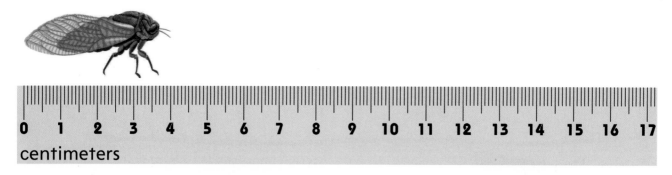

The insect is about 4 centimeters long. We write this as 4 cm.

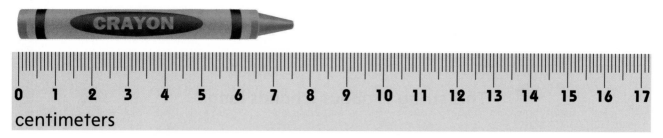

The crayon is about $7\frac{1}{2}$ centimeters long. We write this as $7\frac{1}{2}$ cm.

Try This!

Measure this pencil. Tell how long it is.

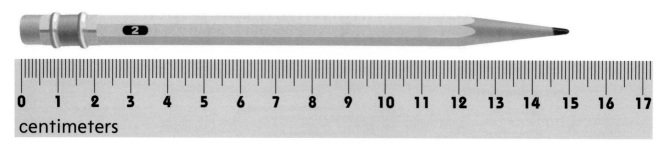

Measure in Inches

You can use inches (in.) to measure, too.
This toy is about $2\frac{1}{2}$ inches, or $2\frac{1}{2}$ in.

Inches

You can estimate how long something is.
When you estimate, you guess the length.
Then you can use a ruler to measure it.

Try This!

Estimate how long each
object is. Then use a ruler
to measure them.

Object	Estimate	Measure
penny	about ____ in.	____ in.
toy car	about ____ in.	____ in.

Use a Measuring Cup

Volume is the amount of space something takes up. You can use a measuring cup to find volume.

You can use different units to measure volume. One unit is called milliliters (mL). Another unit is called a cup. Two cups make up a pint.

Try This!

- Find a container. Estimate how much water it can hold.

- Then fill it with water. Measure the water in milliliters or cups to find out if you were right.

Use a Balance

A balance compares masses.

Place one object on each side of the balance. The object that has more mass will make that side of the balance go down. The object that has less mass will go up.

Try This!

- Place 2 objects on a balance. Which has more mass?

- Put 3 objects in order from least mass to most mass. Use the balance to check.

Before you compare masses, make sure the arrow points to the line.

Use a Scale

A scale measures weight. As an animal grows, it gets bigger and gains weight. You can measure weight in pounds (lbs).

Try This!

- What is your weight? First, estimate your weight. Then, use a scale to measure it.

- Every month, measure your weight. Record it in a chart. See how your weight changes as you grow.

Use a Thermometer

A thermometer measures temperature.
There is liquid inside the thermometer.

When it gets warmer, the liquid
moves up.

When it gets cooler, the liquid
moves down.

Which thermometer shows a warmer
temperature? How can you tell?

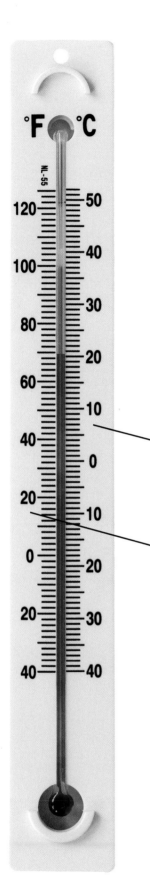

A thermometer measures temperature in degrees. The marks show degrees Fahrenheit and degrees Celsius.

Read this thermometer in degrees Celsius. Look at the numbers on the right side. Find the number where the liquid ends.

degrees Celsius

degrees Fahrenheit

Try This!

Read the thermometers on page R24. What temperatures are shown?

Use Weather Tools

You can use weather tools to measure the weather. A thermometer tells you how hot or cool the air is outside.

A rain gauge tells you how much rain falls. It has a jar that catches the rain. It also has a ruler to measure how much rain falls into the jar.

weather vane

rain gauge

wind sock

A wind sock and weather vane tell which way the wind blows. The arrow on a weather vane tells where the wind is coming from. It points to the north, south, east, or west.

An anemometer measures how fast the wind blows. It tells you the wind's speed.

Try This!

Use a rain gauge. Measure how much rain falls on two different days that rain. Compare the amounts.

anemometer

Use a Clock

A clock measures time.

minute hand

hour hand

The numbers tell what hour it is.

There are 5 minutes between each number.

There are 60 minutes in 1 hour.

1:30

30 minutes after 1 o'clock

9:05

5 minutes after 9 o'clock

Try This!

Estimate how long you sleep each night.
Use a clock to find out.

Use a Hand Lens

A hand lens makes objects seem larger.

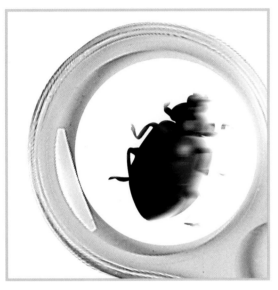

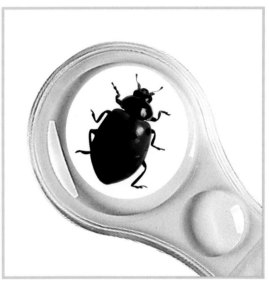

First, move the lens away from the object. Stop when the object looks fuzzy.

Next, move the lens a little closer to the object. Stop when the object looks clear.

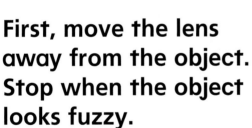

- Observe each bug here. Use a hand lens.

- How many legs do you see on the bugs?

- What else can you see?

Use a Computer

You can use a computer to get information.

You can use CD-ROMs. They save a lot of information. You can fit many books on one CD-ROM!

You can also use the Internet. The Internet links your computer to ones far away.

Try This!

Visit **www.science.mmhschool.com** to find out more about science in your world.

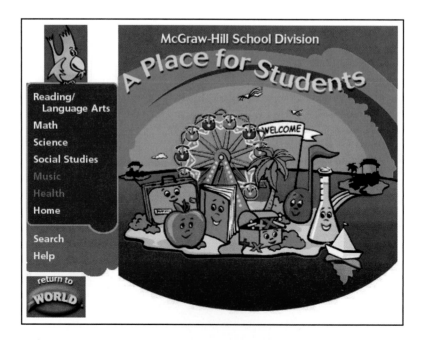

Your Body

Each part of your body has a job to do.

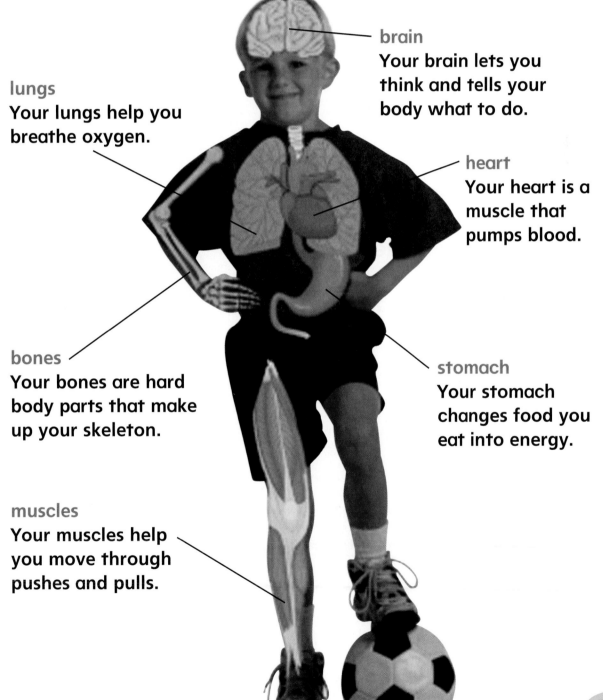

brain
Your brain lets you think and tells your body what to do.

lungs
Your lungs help you breathe oxygen.

heart
Your heart is a muscle that pumps blood.

bones
Your bones are hard body parts that make up your skeleton.

stomach
Your stomach changes food you eat into energy.

muscles
Your muscles help you move through pushes and pulls.

Take Care of Your Body

Keep your body clean.

Brush and floss your teeth.

Take care of your hair and nails.

Sit and stand up tall.

Wash your hands before and after you eat.

Germs are on things you touch.
Germs can make you sick.

Wash your hands often.

Eat Healthful Foods

Healthful foods give your body energy. You use energy to walk, play, and move. You need energy to help you grow and stay healthy.

Choose healthful foods.

Milk helps your teeth and bones grow.

Fruits and vegetables give you energy.
Bread and cereal do, too.

Meat helps your muscles grow.

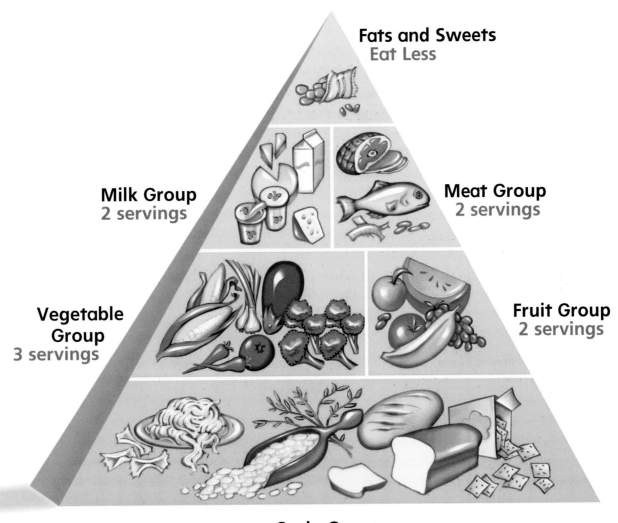

Fats and Sweets
Eat Less

Milk Group
2 servings

Meat Group
2 servings

Vegetable Group
3 servings

Fruit Group
2 servings

Grain Group
6 servings

Be Active and Rest

Be active every day.
When you are active,
your heart beats faster.
This keeps you healthy
and strong.

Get plenty of
sleep at night.

These things
help you grow!

Stay Healthy

Your body grows and changes.

Get checkups every year.

Doctors and dentists can help you stay healthy as you grow. They can help you get better when you are sick.

Be Safe Indoors

Some things are dangerous. Don't touch them!
Tell an adult when you find something dangerous.

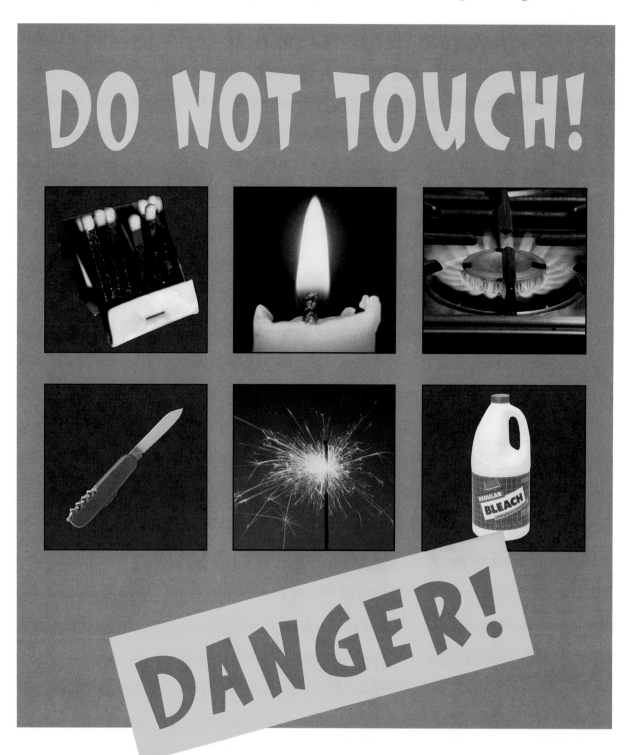

Be Safe Outdoors

Getting Along

Work and play well with others.

Respect one another's feelings.

Show others that you care.